City

DESTINATION:

SPECIAL EVENTS:

DAYS: WEATHER:

Basics

ESSENTIALS	ELECTRONICS
Passport (with visa if necessary)	Camera and charger
	Mobile phone and charger
Driving license	
Boarding passes/tickets	Tablet and charger
Foreign cash	Headphones
Credit/ATM cards	Plug adapters
Pocket city guidebook	
Maps/directions/itinerary	
Small combination lock	
Travel insurance documents	
Repeat and travel medication	
Small day handbag/backpack	
Small case with wheels	

Clothes

Light jacket	Sandals
Waterproof coat	Smart shoes
Light jumpers/cardigans	Trainers/leisure shoes
Casual shirts	Scar
Vest tops	Belt
T-shirts	Soc
Jeans	Und
Smart trousers	Tigh
Loose trousers	Sleep
Leggings	Jewe
Shorts	Sung
Skirts	Cap/
Day dresses	Swim
Evening dresses	

'HE WHO WOULD TRAVEL HAPPILY MUST TRAVEL LIGH

	DESTINATION:
	SPECIAL EVENTS:
	DAYS: WEATHER:

	ESSENTIALS	
Hygiene	Suncream and aftersun lotion	Hairbrush/comb
	Body lotion/moisturiser	Hair products
	Insect repellent	Disposable wipes
	Deodorant	Sanitary products
	Small perfume sticks	Nail file/clippers
	Razor and shaving cream	Tweezers
	Toothbrush	Hand sanitizer
	Toothpaste	
	Make-up and remover	
Miscellaneous	Travel pillow and blanket	
	Painkillers	
	Glasses	
	Contact lenses & solution	
	Travel journal and pen	
	Books	

'HE WHO WOULD TRAVEL HAPPILY MUST TRAVEL LIGHT' ANTOINE DE ST-EXUPERY

City

DESTINATION:
SPECIAL EVENTS:
DAYS: WEATHER:

Basics	ESSENTIALS	ELECTRONICS
	Passport (with visa if necessary)	Camera and charger
	Driving license	Mobile phone and charger
	Boarding passes/tickets	Tablet and charger
	Foreign cash	Headphones
	Credit/ATM cards	Plug adapters
	Pocket city guidebook	
	Maps/directions/itinerary	
	Small combination lock	
	Travel insurance documents	
	Repeat and travel medication	
	Small day handbag/backpack	
	Small case with wheels	

Clothes		
	Light jacket	Sandals
	Waterproof coat	Smart shoes
	Light jumpers/cardigans	Trainers/leisure shoes
	Casual shirts	Scarf/shawl
	Vest tops	Belt
	T-shirts	Socks
	Jeans	Underwear
	Smart trousers	Tights
	Loose trousers	Sleepwear
	Leggings	Jewellery
	Shorts	Sunglasses
	Skirts	Cap/hat
	Day dresses	Swimsuit
	Evening dresses	

'HE WHO WOULD TRAVEL HAPPILY MUST TRAVEL LIGHT' ANTOINE DE ST-EXUPERY

		DESTINATION:
		SPECIAL EVENTS:
		DAYS: WEATHER:

	ESSENTIALS	
Hygiene	Suncream and aftersun	Hairbrush/comb
	lotion	Hair products
	Body lotion/moisturiser	Disposable wipes
	Insect repellent	Sanitary products
	Deodorant	Nail file/clippers
	Small perfume sticks	Tweezers
	Razor and shaving cream	Hand sanitizer
	Toothbrush	
	Toothpaste	
	Make-up and remover	
Miscellaneous	Travel pillow and blanket	
	Painkillers	
	Glasses	
	Contact lenses & solution	
	Travel journal and pen	
	Books	

'HE WHO WOULD TRAVEL HAPPILY MUST TRAVEL LIGHT' ANTOINE DE ST-EXUPERY

City

DESTINATION:

SPECIAL EVENTS:

DAYS: **WEATHER:**

Basics

ESSENTIALS	ELECTRONICS
Passport (with visa if necessary)	Camera and charger
	Mobile phone and charger
Driving license	
Boarding passes/tickets	Tablet and charger
Foreign cash	Headphones
Credit/ATM cards	Plug adapters
Pocket city guidebook	
Maps/directions/itinerary	
Small combination lock	
Travel insurance documents	
Repeat and travel medication	
Small day handbag/backpack	
Small case with wheels	

Clothes

Light jacket	Sandals
Waterproof coat	Smart shoes
Light jumpers/cardigans	Trainers/leisure shoes
Casual shirts	Scarf/shawl
Vest tops	Belt
T-shirts	Socks
Jeans	Underwear
Smart trousers	Tights
Loose trousers	Sleepwear
Leggings	Jewellery
Shorts	Sunglasses
Skirts	Cap/hat
Day dresses	Swimsuit
Evening dresses	

'HE WHO WOULD TRAVEL HAPPILY MUST TRAVEL LIGHT' ANTOINE DE ST-EXUPERY

		DESTINATION:
		SPECIAL EVENTS:
		DAYS: WEATHER:

	ESSENTIALS	
	Suncream and aftersun	Hairbrush/comb
	lotion	Hair products
	Body lotion/moisturiser	Disposable wipes
	Insect repellent	Sanitary products
Hygiene	Deodorant	Nail file/clippers
	Small perfume sticks	Tweezers
	Razor and shaving cream	Hand sanitizer
	Toothbrush	
	Toothpaste	
	Make-up and remover	
	Travel pillow and blanket	
	Painkillers	
	Glasses	
Miscellaneous	Contact lenses & solution	
	Travel journal and pen	
	Books	

'HE WHO WOULD TRAVEL HAPPILY MUST TRAVEL LIGHT' ANTOINE DE ST-EXUPERY

City

DESTINATION:

SPECIAL EVENTS:

DAYS: WEATHER:

Basics	ESSENTIALS	ELECTRONICS
	Passport (with visa if necessary)	Camera and charger
		Mobile phone and charger
	Driving license	
	Boarding passes/tickets	Tablet and charger
	Foreign cash	Headphones
	Credit/ATM cards	Plug adapters
	Pocket city guidebook	
	Maps/directions/itinerary	
	Small combination lock	
	Travel insurance documents	
	Repeat and travel medication	
	Small day handbag/backpack	
	Small case with wheels	

Clothes		
	Light jacket	Sandals
	Waterproof coat	Smart shoes
	Light jumpers/cardigans	Trainers/leisure shoes
	Casual shirts	Scarf/shawl
	Vest tops	Belt
	T-shirts	Socks
	Jeans	Underwear
	Smart trousers	Tights
	Loose trousers	Sleepwear
	Leggings	Jewellery
	Shorts	Sunglasses
	Skirts	Cap/hat
	Day dresses	Swimsuit
	Evening dresses	

'HE WHO WOULD TRAVEL HAPPILY MUST TRAVEL LIGHT' ANTOINE DE ST-EXUPERY

	DESTINATION:
	SPECIAL EVENTS:
	DAYS: WEATHER:

	ESSENTIALS	
Hygiene	Suncream and aftersun lotion	Hairbrush/comb
	Body lotion/moisturiser	Hair products
	Insect repellent	Disposable wipes
	Deodorant	Sanitary products
	Small perfume sticks	Nail file/clippers
	Razor and shaving cream	Tweezers
	Toothbrush	Hand sanitizer
	Toothpaste	
	Make-up and remover	
Miscellaneous	Travel pillow and blanket	
	Painkillers	
	Glasses	
	Contact lenses & solution	
	Travel journal and pen	
	Books	

'HE WHO WOULD TRAVEL HAPPILY MUST TRAVEL LIGHT' ANTOINE DE ST-EXUPERY

City

DESTINATION:

SPECIAL EVENTS:

DAYS: WEATHER:

	ESSENTIALS	ELECTRONICS
Basics	Passport (with visa if necessary)	Camera and charger
	Driving license	Mobile phone and charger
	Boarding passes/tickets	Tablet and charger
	Foreign cash	Headphones
	Credit/ATM cards	Plug adapters
	Pocket city guidebook	
	Maps/directions/itinerary	
	Small combination lock	
	Travel insurance documents	
	Repeat and travel medication	
	Small day handbag/backpack	
	Small case with wheels	
Clothes	Light jacket	Sandals
	Waterproof coat	Smart shoes
	Light jumpers/cardigans	Trainers/leisure shoes
	Casual shirts	Scarf/shawl
	Vest tops	Belt
	T-shirts	Socks
	Jeans	Underwear
	Smart trousers	Tights
	Loose trousers	Sleepwear
	Leggings	Jewellery
	Shorts	Sunglasses
	Skirts	Cap/hat
	Day dresses	Swimsuit
	Evening dresses	

'HE WHO WOULD TRAVEL HAPPILY MUST TRAVEL LIGHT' ANTOINE DE ST-EXUPERY

		DESTINATION:
		SPECIAL EVENTS:
		DAYS: WEATHER:

	ESSENTIALS	
Hygiene	Suncream and aftersun lotion	Hairbrush/comb
	Body lotion/moisturiser	Hair products
	Insect repellent	Disposable wipes
	Deodorant	Sanitary products
	Small perfume sticks	Nail file/clippers
	Razor and shaving cream	Tweezers
	Toothbrush	Hand sanitizer
	Toothpaste	
	Make-up and remover	
Miscellaneous	Travel pillow and blanket	
	Painkillers	
	Glasses	
	Contact lenses & solution	
	Travel journal and pen	
	Books	

'HE WHO WOULD TRAVEL HAPPILY MUST TRAVEL LIGHT' ANTOINE DE ST-EXUPERY

City

DESTINATION:
SPECIAL EVENTS:
DAYS: WEATHER:

Basics

ESSENTIALS	ELECTRONICS
Passport (with visa if necessary)	Camera and charger
Driving license	Mobile phone and charger
Boarding passes/tickets	Tablet and charger
Foreign cash	Headphones
Credit/ATM cards	Plug adapters
Pocket city guidebook	
Maps/directions/itinerary	
Small combination lock	
Travel insurance documents	
Repeat and travel medication	
Small day handbag/backpack	
Small case with wheels	

Clothes

Light jacket	Sandals
Waterproof coat	Smart shoes
Light jumpers/cardigans	Trainers/leisure shoes
Casual shirts	Scarf/shawl
Vest tops	Belt
T-shirts	Socks
Jeans	Underwear
Smart trousers	Tights
Loose trousers	Sleepwear
Leggings	Jewellery
Shorts	Sunglasses
Skirts	Cap/hat
Day dresses	Swimsuit
Evening dresses	

'HE WHO WOULD TRAVEL HAPPILY MUST TRAVEL LIGHT' ANTOINE DE ST-EXUPERY

		DESTINATION:
		SPECIAL EVENTS:
		DAYS: WEATHER:

	ESSENTIALS	
Hygiene	Suncream and aftersun lotion	Hairbrush/comb
	Body lotion/moisturiser	Hair products
	Insect repellent	Disposable wipes
	Deodorant	Sanitary products
	Small perfume sticks	Nail file/clippers
	Razor and shaving cream	Tweezers
	Toothbrush	Hand sanitizer
	Toothpaste	
	Make-up and remover	
Miscellaneous	Travel pillow and blanket	
	Painkillers	
	Glasses	
	Contact lenses & solution	
	Travel journal and pen	
	Books	

'HE WHO WOULD TRAVEL HAPPILY MUST TRAVEL LIGHT' ANTOINE DE ST-EXUPERY

City

DESTINATION:

SPECIAL EVENTS:

DAYS: WEATHER:

	ESSENTIALS	ELECTRONICS
Basics	Passport (with visa if necessary)	Camera and charger
	Driving license	Mobile phone and charger
	Boarding passes/tickets	Tablet and charger
	Foreign cash	Headphones
	Credit/ATM cards	Plug adapters
	Pocket city guidebook	
	Maps/directions/itinerary	
	Small combination lock	
	Travel insurance documents	
	Repeat and travel medication	
	Small day handbag/backpack	
	Small case with wheels	
Clothes	Light jacket	Sandals
	Waterproof coat	Smart shoes
	Light jumpers/cardigans	Trainers/leisure shoes
	Casual shirts	Scarf/shawl
	Vest tops	Belt
	T-shirts	Socks
	Jeans	Underwear
	Smart trousers	Tights
	Loose trousers	Sleepwear
	Leggings	Jewellery
	Shorts	Sunglasses
	Skirts	Cap/hat
	Day dresses	Swimsuit
	Evening dresses	

'HE WHO WOULD TRAVEL HAPPILY MUST TRAVEL LIGHT' ANTOINE DE ST-EXUPERY

		DESTINATION:
		SPECIAL EVENTS:
		DAYS: WEATHER:

	ESSENTIALS	
Hygiene	Suncream and aftersun	Hairbrush/comb
	lotion	Hair products
	Body lotion/moisturiser	Disposable wipes
	Insect repellent	Sanitary products
	Deodorant	Nail file/clippers
	Small perfume sticks	Tweezers
	Razor and shaving cream	Hand sanitizer
	Toothbrush	
	Toothpaste	
	Make-up and remover	
Miscellaneous	Travel pillow and blanket	
	Painkillers	
	Glasses	
	Contact lenses & solution	
	Travel journal and pen	
	Books	

'HE WHO WOULD TRAVEL HAPPILY MUST TRAVEL LIGHT' ANTOINE DE ST-EXUPERY

City		DESTINATION: SPECIAL EVENTS: DAYS: WEATHER:

	ESSENTIALS	**ELECTRONICS**
Basics	Passport (with visa if necessary)	Camera and charger
	Driving license	Mobile phone and charger
	Boarding passes/tickets	Tablet and charger
	Foreign cash	Headphones
	Credit/ATM cards	Plug adapters
	Pocket city guidebook	
	Maps/directions/itinerary	
	Small combination lock	
	Travel insurance documents	
	Repeat and travel medication	
	Small day handbag/backpack	
	Small case with wheels	
Clothes	Light jacket	Sandals
	Waterproof coat	Smart shoes
	Light jumpers/cardigans	Trainers/leisure shoes
	Casual shirts	Scarf/shawl
	Vest tops	Belt
	T-shirts	Socks
	Jeans	Underwear
	Smart trousers	Tights
	Loose trousers	Sleepwear
	Leggings	Jewellery
	Shorts	Sunglasses
	Skirts	Cap/hat
	Day dresses	Swimsuit
	Evening dresses	

'HE WHO WOULD TRAVEL HAPPILY MUST TRAVEL LIGHT' ANTOINE DE ST-EXUPERY

		DESTINATION:
		SPECIAL EVENTS:
		DAYS: WEATHER:

	ESSENTIALS	
Hygiene	Suncream and aftersun	Hairbrush/comb
	lotion	Hair products
	Body lotion/moisturiser	Disposable wipes
	Insect repellent	Sanitary products
	Deodorant	Nail file/clippers
	Small perfume sticks	Tweezers
	Razor and shaving cream	Hand sanitizer
	Toothbrush	
	Toothpaste	
	Make-up and remover	
Miscellaneous	Travel pillow and blanket	
	Painkillers	
	Glasses	
	Contact lenses & solution	
	Travel journal and pen	
	Books	

'HE WHO WOULD TRAVEL HAPPILY MUST TRAVEL LIGHT' ANTOINE DE ST-EXUPERY

City	DESTINATION:
	SPECIAL EVENTS:
	DAYS: WEATHER:

	ESSENTIALS	ELECTRONICS
Basics	Passport (with visa if necessary)	Camera and charger
	Driving license	Mobile phone and charger
	Boarding passes/tickets	Tablet and charger
	Foreign cash	Headphones
	Credit/ATM cards	Plug adapters
	Pocket city guidebook	
	Maps/directions/itinerary	
	Small combination lock	
	Travel insurance documents	
	Repeat and travel medication	
	Small day handbag/backpack	
	Small case with wheels	
Clothes	Light jacket	Sandals
	Waterproof coat	Smart shoes
	Light jumpers/cardigans	Trainers/leisure shoes
	Casual shirts	Scarf/shawl
	Vest tops	Belt
	T-shirts	Socks
	Jeans	Underwear
	Smart trousers	Tights
	Loose trousers	Sleepwear
	Leggings	Jewellery
	Shorts	Sunglasses
	Skirts	Cap/hat
	Day dresses	Swimsuit
	Evening dresses	

'HE WHO WOULD TRAVEL HAPPILY MUST TRAVEL LIGHT' ANTOINE DE ST-EXUPERY

	DESTINATION:
	SPECIAL EVENTS:
	DAYS: WEATHER:

ESSENTIALS

Hygiene

Suncream and aftersun lotion	Hairbrush/comb
Body lotion/moisturiser	Hair products
Insect repellent	Disposable wipes
Deodorant	Sanitary products
Small perfume sticks	Nail file/clippers
Razor and shaving cream	Tweezers
Toothbrush	Hand sanitizer
Toothpaste	
Make-up and remover	

Miscellaneous

Travel pillow and blanket	
Painkillers	
Glasses	
Contact lenses & solution	
Travel journal and pen	
Books	

'HE WHO WOULD TRAVEL HAPPILY MUST TRAVEL LIGHT' ANTOINE DE ST-EXUPERY

Beach

DESTINATION:
SPECIAL EVENTS:
DAYS: WEATHER:

	ESSENTIALS	ELECTRONICS
Basics	Passport (with visa if necessary)	Camera and charger
	Driving license	Mobile phone and charger
	Boarding passes/tickets	Tablet and charger
	Foreign cash	Headphones
	Credit/ATM cards	Plug adapters
	Book(s)	
	Maps/directions/itinerary	
	First aid kit	
	Travel insurance documents	
	Repeat & travel medication	
	Suitcase/backpack	
Clothes	Swimsuit	Flip-flops
	Sarong/shawl	Trainers/leisure shoes
	Light jacket	Belt
	Waterproof coat	Socks
	Light jumpers	Underwear
	Casual shirts	Tights
	Vest tops	Sleepwear
	T-shirts	Jewellery
	Jeans	Sunglasses
	Smart trousers	Sun hat
	Loose trousers	Waterproof watch
	Leggings	
	Shorts	
	Skirts	
	Day dresses	
	Evening dresses	
	Sandals	
	Smart shoes	

'HE WHO WOULD TRAVEL HAPPILY MUST TRAVEL LIGHT' ANTOINE DE ST-EXUPERY

	DESTINATION:
	SPECIAL EVENTS:
	DAYS: WEATHER:

	ESSENTIALS	
Hygiene	Suncream and aftersun lotion	Toothpaste
	Body lotion/moisturiser	Make-up and remover
	Insect repellent	Hairbrush/comb
	Deodorant	Hair products
	Perfume	Disposable wipes
	SPF lip balm	Sanitary products
	Razor and shaving cream	Nail file/clippers
	Shampoo and conditioner	Tweezers
	Soap/body wash	Bug spray
	Toothbrush	Talc (for getting sand off)

Miscellaneous	Travel pillow and blanket	
	Painkillers	
	Glasses	
	Contact lenses & solution	
	Travel journal and pen	
	Goggles/snorkel and fins	
	Water shoes	
	Swimming cap	
	Books	
	Beach chairs	
	Beach bag	
	Beach towel/quick-dry towel	
	UV tent/sunshade	
	Bucket and spade	
	Picnic box/bag	
	Blanket/picnic rug	

'HE WHO WOULD TRAVEL HAPPILY MUST TRAVEL LIGHT' ANTOINE DE ST-EXUPERY

Beach

DESTINATION:

SPECIAL EVENTS:

DAYS: WEATHER:

Basics

ESSENTIALS	ELECTRONICS
Passport (with visa if necessary)	Camera and charger
Driving license	Mobile phone and charger
Boarding passes/tickets	Tablet and charger
Foreign cash	Headphones
Credit/ATM cards	Plug adapters
Book(s)	
Maps/directions/itinerary	
First aid kit	
Travel insurance documents	
Repeat & travel medication	
Suitcase/backpack	

Clothes

Swimsuit	Flip-flops
Sarong/shawl	Trainers/leisure shoes
Light jacket	Belt
Waterproof coat	Socks
Light jumpers	Underwear
Casual shirts	Tights
Vest tops	Sleepwear
T-shirts	Jewellery
Jeans	Sunglasses
Smart trousers	Sun hat
Loose trousers	Waterproof watch
Leggings	
Shorts	
Skirts	
Day dresses	
Evening dresses	
Sandals	
Smart shoes	

'HE WHO WOULD TRAVEL HAPPILY MUST TRAVEL LIGHT' ANTOINE DE ST-EXUPERY

		DESTINATION:
		SPECIAL EVENTS:
		DAYS: WEATHER:
	ESSENTIALS	
Hygiene	Suncream and aftersun lotion	Toothpaste
	Body lotion/moisturiser	Make-up and remover
	Insect repellent	Hairbrush/comb
	Deodorant	Hair products
	Perfume	Disposable wipes
	SPF lip balm	Sanitary products
	Razor and shaving cream	Nail file/clippers
	Shampoo and conditioner	Tweezers
	Soap/body wash	Bug spray
	Toothbrush	Talc (for getting sand off)
Miscellaneous	Travel pillow and blanket	
	Painkillers	
	Glasses	
	Contact lenses & solution	
	Travel journal and pen	
	Goggles/snorkel and fins	
	Water shoes	
	Swimming cap	
	Books	
	Beach chairs	
	Beach bag	
	Beach towel/quick-dry towel	
	UV tent/sunshade	
	Bucket and spade	
	Picnic box/bag	
	Blanket/picnic rug	

'HE WHO WOULD TRAVEL HAPPILY MUST TRAVEL LIGHT' ANTOINE DE ST-EXUPERY

Beach

DESTINATION:

SPECIAL EVENTS:

DAYS: WEATHER:

Basics	ESSENTIALS	ELECTRONICS
	Passport (with visa if necessary)	Camera and charger
		Mobile phone and charger
	Driving license	
	Boarding passes/tickets	Tablet and charger
	Foreign cash	Headphones
	Credit/ATM cards	Plug adapters
	Book(s)	
	Maps/directions/itinerary	
	First aid kit	
	Travel insurance documents	
	Repeat & travel medication	
	Suitcase/backpack	

Clothes		
	Swimsuit	Flip-flops
	Sarong/shawl	Trainers/leisure shoes
	Light jacket	Belt
	Waterproof coat	Socks
	Light jumpers	Underwear
	Casual shirts	Tights
	Vest tops	Sleepwear
	T-shirts	Jewellery
	Jeans	Sunglasses
	Smart trousers	Sun hat
	Loose trousers	Waterproof watch
	Leggings	
	Shorts	
	Skirts	
	Day dresses	
	Evening dresses	
	Sandals	
	Smart shoes	

'HE WHO WOULD TRAVEL HAPPILY MUST TRAVEL LIGHT' ANTOINE DE ST-EXUPERY

		DESTINATION:
		SPECIAL EVENTS:
		DAYS: WEATHER:

	ESSENTIALS	
Hygiene	Suncream and aftersun	Toothpaste
	lotion	Make-up and remover
	Body lotion/moisturiser	Hairbrush/comb
	Insect repellent	Hair products
	Deodorant	Disposable wipes
	Perfume	Sanitary products
	SPF lip balm	Nail file/clippers
	Razor and shaving cream	Tweezers
	Shampoo and conditioner	Bug spray
	Soap/body wash	Talc (for getting sand off)
	Toothbrush	
Miscellaneous	Travel pillow and blanket	
	Painkillers	
	Glasses	
	Contact lenses & solution	
	Travel journal and pen	
	Goggles/snorkel and fins	
	Water shoes	
	Swimming cap	
	Books	
	Beach chairs	
	Beach bag	
	Beach towel/quick-dry	
	towel	
	UV tent/sunshade	
	Bucket and spade	
	Picnic box/bag	
	Blanket/picnic rug	

'HE WHO WOULD TRAVEL HAPPILY MUST TRAVEL LIGHT' ANTOINE DE ST-EXUPERY

Beach

DESTINATION:

SPECIAL EVENTS:

DAYS: WEATHER:

Basics

ESSENTIALS	ELECTRONICS
Passport (with visa if necessary)	Camera and charger
Driving license	Mobile phone and charger
Boarding passes/tickets	Tablet and charger
Foreign cash	Headphones
Credit/ATM cards	Plug adapters
Book(s)	
Maps/directions/itinerary	
First aid kit	
Travel insurance documents	
Repeat & travel medication	
Suitcase/backpack	

Clothes

Swimsuit	Flip-flops
Sarong/shawl	Trainers/leisure shoes
Light jacket	Belt
Waterproof coat	Socks
Light jumpers	Underwear
Casual shirts	Tights
Vest tops	Sleepwear
T-shirts	Jewellery
Jeans	Sunglasses
Smart trousers	Sun hat
Loose trousers	Waterproof watch
Leggings	
Shorts	
Skirts	
Day dresses	
Evening dresses	
Sandals	
Smart shoes	

'HE WHO WOULD TRAVEL HAPPILY MUST TRAVEL LIGHT' ANTOINE DE ST-EXUPERY

		DESTINATION:
		SPECIAL EVENTS:
		DAYS: WEATHER:

	ESSENTIALS	
Hygiene	Suncream and aftersun lotion	Toothpaste
	Body lotion/moisturiser	Make-up and remover
	Insect repellent	Hairbrush/comb
	Deodorant	Hair products
	Perfume	Disposable wipes
	SPF lip balm	Sanitary products
	Razor and shaving cream	Nail file/clippers
	Shampoo and conditioner	Tweezers
	Soap/body wash	Bug spray
	Toothbrush	Talc (for getting sand off)
Miscellaneous	Travel pillow and blanket	
	Painkillers	
	Glasses	
	Contact lenses & solution	
	Travel journal and pen	
	Goggles/snorkel and fins	
	Water shoes	
	Swimming cap	
	Books	
	Beach chairs	
	Beach bag	
	Beach towel/quick-dry towel	
	UV tent/sunshade	
	Bucket and spade	
	Picnic box/bag	
	Blanket/picnic rug	

'HE WHO WOULD TRAVEL HAPPILY MUST TRAVEL LIGHT' ANTOINE DE ST-EXUPERY

Beach

DESTINATION:

SPECIAL EVENTS:

DAYS: WEATHER:

	ESSENTIALS	ELECTRONICS
Basics	Passport (with visa if necessary)	Camera and charger
	Driving license	Mobile phone and charger
	Boarding passes/tickets	Tablet and charger
	Foreign cash	Headphones
	Credit/ATM cards	Plug adapters
	Book(s)	
	Maps/directions/itinerary	
	First aid kit	
	Travel insurance documents	
	Repeat & travel medication	
	Suitcase/backpack	
Clothes	Swimsuit	Flip-flops
	Sarong/shawl	Trainers/leisure shoes
	Light jacket	Belt
	Waterproof coat	Socks
	Light jumpers	Underwear
	Casual shirts	Tights
	Vest tops	Sleepwear
	T-shirts	Jewellery
	Jeans	Sunglasses
	Smart trousers	Sun hat
	Loose trousers	Waterproof watch
	Leggings	
	Shorts	
	Skirts	
	Day dresses	
	Evening dresses	
	Sandals	
	Smart shoes	

'HE WHO WOULD TRAVEL HAPPILY MUST TRAVEL LIGHT' ANTOINE DE ST-EXUPERY

		DESTINATION:
		SPECIAL EVENTS:
		DAYS: WEATHER:
	ESSENTIALS	
Hygiene	Suncream and aftersun	Toothpaste
	lotion	Make-up and remover
	Body lotion/moisturiser	Hairbrush/comb
	Insect repellent	Hair products
	Deodorant	Disposable wipes
	Perfume	Sanitary products
	SPF lip balm	Nail file/clippers
	Razor and shaving cream	Tweezers
	Shampoo and conditioner	Bug spray
	Soap/body wash	Talc (for getting sand off)
	Toothbrush	
Miscellaneous	Travel pillow and blanket	
	Painkillers	
	Glasses	
	Contact lenses & solution	
	Travel journal and pen	
	Goggles/snorkel and fins	
	Water shoes	
	Swimming cap	
	Books	
	Beach chairs	
	Beach bag	
	Beach towel/quick-dry	
	towel	
	UV tent/sunshade	
	Bucket and spade	
	Picnic box/bag	
	Blanket/picnic rug	

'HE WHO WOULD TRAVEL HAPPILY MUST TRAVEL LIGHT' ANTOINE DE ST-EXUPERY

Beach		DESTINATION: SPECIAL EVENTS: DAYS: WEATHER:

	ESSENTIALS	**ELECTRONICS**
Basics	Passport (with visa if necessary)	Camera and charger
	Driving license	Mobile phone and charger
	Boarding passes/tickets	Tablet and charger
	Foreign cash	Headphones
	Credit/ATM cards	Plug adapters
	Book(s)	
	Maps/directions/itinerary	
	First aid kit	
	Travel insurance documents	
	Repeat & travel medication	
	Suitcase/backpack	
Clothes	Swimsuit	Flip-flops
	Sarong/shawl	Trainers/leisure shoes
	Light jacket	Belt
	Waterproof coat	Socks
	Light jumpers	Underwear
	Casual shirts	Tights
	Vest tops	Sleepwear
	T-shirts	Jewellery
	Jeans	Sunglasses
	Smart trousers	Sun hat
	Loose trousers	Waterproof watch
	Leggings	
	Shorts	
	Skirts	
	Day dresses	
	Evening dresses	
	Sandals	
	Smart shoes	

'HE WHO WOULD TRAVEL HAPPILY MUST TRAVEL LIGHT' ANTOINE DE ST-EXUPERY

		DESTINATION:
		SPECIAL EVENTS:
		DAYS: WEATHER:
	ESSENTIALS	
Hygiene	Suncream and aftersun	Toothpaste
	lotion	Make-up and remover
	Body lotion/moisturiser	Hairbrush/comb
	Insect repellent	Hair products
	Deodorant	Disposable wipes
	Perfume	Sanitary products
	SPF lip balm	Nail file/clippers
	Razor and shaving cream	Tweezers
	Shampoo and conditioner	Bug spray
	Soap/body wash	Talc (for getting sand off)
	Toothbrush	
Miscellaneous	Travel pillow and blanket	
	Painkillers	
	Glasses	
	Contact lenses & solution	
	Travel journal and pen	
	Goggles/snorkel and fins	
	Water shoes	
	Swimming cap	
	Books	
	Beach chairs	
	Beach bag	
	Beach towel/quick-dry	
	towel	
	UV tent/sunshade	
	Bucket and spade	
	Picnic box/bag	
	Blanket/picnic rug	

'HE WHO WOULD TRAVEL HAPPILY MUST TRAVEL LIGHT' ANTOINE DE ST-EXUPERY

Beach

Basics

ESSENTIALS	ELECTRONICS
Passport (with visa if necessary)	Camera and charger
Driving license	Mobile phone and charger
Boarding passes/tickets	Tablet and charger
Foreign cash	Headphones
Credit/ATM cards	Plug adapters
Book(s)	
Maps/directions/itinerary	
First aid kit	
Travel insurance documents	
Repeat & travel medication	
Suitcase/backpack	

Clothes

Swimsuit	Flip-flops
Sarong/shawl	Trainers/leisure shoes
Light jacket	Belt
Waterproof coat	Socks
Light jumpers	Underwear
Casual shirts	Tights
Vest tops	Sleepwear
T-shirts	Jewellery
Jeans	Sunglasses
Smart trousers	Sun hat
Loose trousers	Waterproof watch
Leggings	
Shorts	
Skirts	
Day dresses	
Evening dresses	
Sandals	
Smart shoes	

'HE WHO WOULD TRAVEL HAPPILY MUST TRAVEL LIGHT' ANTOINE DE ST-EXUPERY

	DESTINATION:
	SPECIAL EVENTS:
	DAYS: WEATHER:

ESSENTIALS

Hygiene

Suncream and aftersun lotion	Toothpaste
Body lotion/moisturiser	Make-up and remover
Insect repellent	Hairbrush/comb
Deodorant	Hair products
Perfume	Disposable wipes
SPF lip balm	Sanitary products
Razor and shaving cream	Nail file/clippers
Shampoo and conditioner	Tweezers
Soap/body wash	Bug spray
Toothbrush	Talc (for getting sand off)

Miscellaneous

Travel pillow and blanket	
Painkillers	
Glasses	
Contact lenses & solution	
Travel journal and pen	
Goggles/snorkel and fins	
Water shoes	
Swimming cap	
Books	
Beach chairs	
Beach bag	
Beach towel/quick-dry towel	
UV tent/sunshade	
Bucket and spade	
Picnic box/bag	
Blanket/picnic rug	

'HE WHO WOULD TRAVEL HAPPILY MUST TRAVEL LIGHT' ANTOINE DE ST-EXUPERY

Beach

DESTINATION:

SPECIAL EVENTS:

DAYS: WEATHER:

Basics

	ESSENTIALS		ELECTRONICS
	Passport (with visa if necessary)		Camera and charger
	Driving license		Mobile phone and charger
	Boarding passes/tickets		Tablet and charger
	Foreign cash		Headphones
	Credit/ATM cards		Plug adapters
	Book(s)		
	Maps/directions/itinerary		
	First aid kit		
	Travel insurance documents		
	Repeat & travel medication		
	Suitcase/backpack		

Clothes

	Swimsuit		Flip-flops
	Sarong/shawl		Trainers/leisure shoes
	Light jacket		Belt
	Waterproof coat		Socks
	Light jumpers		Underwear
	Casual shirts		Tights
	Vest tops		Sleepwear
	T-shirts		Jewellery
	Jeans		Sunglasses
	Smart trousers		Sun hat
	Loose trousers		Waterproof watch
	Leggings		
	Shorts		
	Skirts		
	Day dresses		
	Evening dresses		
	Sandals		
	Smart shoes		

'HE WHO WOULD TRAVEL HAPPILY MUST TRAVEL LIGHT' ANTOINE DE ST-EXUPERY

		DESTINATION:
		SPECIAL EVENTS:
		DAYS: WEATHER:

	ESSENTIALS	
Hygiene	Suncream and aftersun	Toothpaste
	lotion	Make-up and remover
	Body lotion/moisturiser	Hairbrush/comb
	Insect repellent	Hair products
	Deodorant	Disposable wipes
	Perfume	Sanitary products
	SPF lip balm	Nail file/clippers
	Razor and shaving cream	Tweezers
	Shampoo and conditioner	Bug spray
	Soap/body wash	Talc (for getting sand off)
	Toothbrush	
Miscellaneous	Travel pillow and blanket	
	Painkillers	
	Glasses	
	Contact lenses & solution	
	Travel journal and pen	
	Goggles/snorkel and fins	
	Water shoes	
	Swimming cap	
	Books	
	Beach chairs	
	Beach bag	
	Beach towel/quick-dry	
	towel	
	UV tent/sunshade	
	Bucket and spade	
	Picnic box/bag	
	Blanket/picnic rug	

'HE WHO WOULD TRAVEL HAPPILY MUST TRAVEL LIGHT' ANTOINE DE ST-EXUPERY

Beach

	ESSENTIALS	ELECTRONICS
Basics	Passport (with visa if necessary)	Camera and charger
	Driving license	Mobile phone and charger
	Boarding passes/tickets	Tablet and charger
	Foreign cash	Headphones
	Credit/ATM cards	Plug adapters
	Book(s)	
	Maps/directions/itinerary	
	First aid kit	
	Travel insurance documents	
	Repeat & travel medication	
	Suitcase/backpack	
Clothes	Swimsuit	Flip-flops
	Sarong/shawl	Trainers/leisure shoes
	Light jacket	Belt
	Waterproof coat	Socks
	Light jumpers	Underwear
	Casual shirts	Tights
	Vest tops	Sleepwear
	T-shirts	Jewellery
	Jeans	Sunglasses
	Smart trousers	Sun hat
	Loose trousers	Waterproof watch
	Leggings	
	Shorts	
	Skirts	
	Day dresses	
	Evening dresses	
	Sandals	
	Smart shoes	

'HE WHO WOULD TRAVEL HAPPILY MUST TRAVEL LIGHT' ANTOINE DE ST-EXUPERY

		DESTINATION:
		SPECIAL EVENTS:
		DAYS: WEATHER:

	ESSENTIALS	
Hygiene	Suncream and aftersun	Toothpaste
	lotion	Make-up and remover
	Body lotion/moisturiser	Hairbrush/comb
	Insect repellent	Hair products
	Deodorant	Disposable wipes
	Perfume	Sanitary products
	SPF lip balm	Nail file/clippers
	Razor and shaving cream	Tweezers
	Shampoo and conditioner	Bug spray
	Soap/body wash	Talc (for getting sand off)
	Toothbrush	
Miscellaneous	Travel pillow and blanket	
	Painkillers	
	Glasses	
	Contact lenses & solution	
	Travel journal and pen	
	Goggles/snorkel and fins	
	Water shoes	
	Swimming cap	
	Books	
	Beach chairs	
	Beach bag	
	Beach towel/quick-dry towel	
	UV tent/sunshade	
	Bucket and spade	
	Picnic box/bag	
	Blanket/picnic rug	

'HE WHO WOULD TRAVEL HAPPILY MUST TRAVEL LIGHT' ANTOINE DE ST-EXUPERY

Adventure	DESTINATION:
	SPECIAL EVENTS:
	DAYS: WEATHER:

	ESSENTIALS	ELECTRONICS
Basics	Passport (with visa if necessary)	Camera and charger
	Driving license	Mobile phone and charger
	Boarding passes/tickets	Tablet and charger
	Foreign cash	Headphones
	Credit/ATM cards	Plug adapters
	Guidebook	Torch/headtorch and batteries
	Maps/directions/itinerary	
	First aid kit	
	Travel insurance documents	
	Repeat and travel medication	
	Backpack/duffel w/outside pockets	
Clothes	Waterproof coat	Smart shoes
	Jumpers/fleeces	Trainers
	Convertible jacket	Water shoes
	Loose shirts	Waterproof watch
	Quick-drying tops	Hidden zipper belt
	T-shirts	Underwear/long underwear
	Cargo trousers	
	Convertible trousers	Sleepwear
	Loose trousers	Wool/thick socks
	Leggings	Warm hat/sun hat
	Shorts	Sunglasses
	Comfortable skirts	Insulating vests/tops
	Comfortable dresses	
	Walking boots	
	Hiking sandals	

'HE WHO WOULD TRAVEL HAPPILY MUST TRAVEL LIGHT' ANTOINE DE ST-EXUPERY

		DESTINATION:
		SPECIAL EVENTS:
		DAYS: WEATHER:

	ESSENTIALS	
Hygiene	Suncream and aftersun	Make-up and remover
	lotion	Hairbrush/comb
	Body lotion/moisturiser	Disposable wipes
	Insect repellent	Sanitary products
	Deodorant	Nail file/clippers
	Perfume	Tweezers
	SPF lip balm	Bug spray
	Razor and shaving cream	Mini-laundry kit: travel
	Shampoo and conditioner	detergent, braided
	Biodegradable soap/body	clothesline, sink-stopper
	wash	
	Toothbrush	
	Toothpaste	
Miscellaneous	Travel pillow and blanket	Waterproof pocket camera
	Painkillers	Sleep sack
	Glasses	Pocket sewing kit
	Contact lenses & solution	Tripod
	Travel journal and pen	Travel alarm clock
	Books	Navigation - GPS/map/
	Sports sunglasses	compass
	Sun hat/cap/bandana	Hydration pack
	Quick-dry towel	Relevant activity equipment
	Water purifying bottle/pills	Refillable waterbottle
	Lighter/matches/flint	
	Waterproof bag	
	Multi-tool	
	Duct tape	
	Emergency whistle	

'HE WHO WOULD TRAVEL HAPPILY MUST TRAVEL LIGHT' ANTOINE DE ST-EXUPERY

Adventure

DESTINATION:

SPECIAL EVENTS:

DAYS: WEATHER:

	ESSENTIALS	ELECTRONICS
Basics	Passport (with visa if necessary)	Camera and charger
	Driving license	Mobile phone and charger
	Boarding passes/tickets	Tablet and charger
	Foreign cash	Headphones
	Credit/ATM cards	Plug adapters
	Guidebook	Torch/headtorch and batteries
	Maps/directions/itinerary	
	First aid kit	
	Travel insurance documents	
	Repeat and travel medication	
	Backpack/duffel w/outside pockets	
Clothes	Waterproof coat	Smart shoes
	Jumpers/fleeces	Trainers
	Convertible jacket	Water shoes
	Loose shirts	Waterproof watch
	Quick-drying tops	Hidden zipper belt
	T-shirts	Underwear/long underwear
	Cargo trousers	
	Convertible trousers	Sleepwear
	Loose trousers	Wool/thick socks
	Leggings	Warm hat/sun hat
	Shorts	Sunglasses
	Comfortable skirts	Insulating vests/tops
	Comfortable dresses	
	Walking boots	
	Hiking sandals	

'HE WHO WOULD TRAVEL HAPPILY MUST TRAVEL LIGHT' ANTOINE DE ST-EXUPERY

	DESTINATION:
	SPECIAL EVENTS:
	DAYS: WEATHER:

	ESSENTIALS	
Hygiene	Suncream and aftersun lotion	Make-up and remover
	Body lotion/moisturiser	Hairbrush/comb
	Insect repellent	Disposable wipes
	Deodorant	Sanitary products
	Perfume	Nail file/clippers
	SPF lip balm	Tweezers
	Razor and shaving cream	Bug spray
	Shampoo and conditioner	Mini-laundry kit: travel
	Biodegradable soap/body wash	detergent, braided
	Toothbrush	clothesline, sink-stopper
	Toothpaste	
Miscellaneous	Travel pillow and blanket	Waterproof pocket camera
	Painkillers	Sleep sack
	Glasses	Pocket sewing kit
	Contact lenses & solution	Tripod
	Travel journal and pen	Travel alarm clock
	Books	Navigation - GPS/map/
	Sports sunglasses	compass
	Sun hat/cap/bandana	Hydration pack
	Quick-dry towel	Relevant activity equipment
	Water purifying bottle/pills	Refillable waterbottle
	Lighter/matches/flint	
	Waterproof bag	
	Multi-tool	
	Duct tape	
	Emergency whistle	

'HE WHO WOULD TRAVEL HAPPILY MUST TRAVEL LIGHT' ANTOINE DE ST-EXUPERY

Adventure

DESTINATION:

SPECIAL EVENTS:

DAYS: WEATHER:

Basics	ESSENTIALS	ELECTRONICS
	Passport (with visa if necessary)	Camera and charger
	Driving license	Mobile phone and charger
	Boarding passes/tickets	Tablet and charger
	Foreign cash	Headphones
	Credit/ATM cards	Plug adapters
	Guidebook	Torch/headtorch and batteries
	Maps/directions/itinerary	
	First aid kit	
	Travel insurance documents	
	Repeat and travel medication	
	Backpack/duffel w/outside pockets	

Clothes		
	Waterproof coat	Smart shoes
	Jumpers/fleeces	Trainers
	Convertible jacket	Water shoes
	Loose shirts	Waterproof watch
	Quick-drying tops	Hidden zipper belt
	T-shirts	Underwear/long under-wear
	Cargo trousers	
	Convertible trousers	Sleepwear
	Loose trousers	Wool/thick socks
	Leggings	Warm hat/sun hat
	Shorts	Sunglasses
	Comfortable skirts	Insulating vests/tops
	Comfortable dresses	
	Walking boots	
	Hiking sandals	

'HE WHO WOULD TRAVEL HAPPILY MUST TRAVEL LIGHT' ANTOINE DE ST-EXUPERY

	DESTINATION:
	SPECIAL EVENTS:
	DAYS: WEATHER:

	ESSENTIALS	
Hygiene	Suncream and aftersun lotion	Make-up and remover
	Body lotion/moisturiser	Hairbrush/comb
	Insect repellent	Disposable wipes
	Deodorant	Sanitary products
	Perfume	Nail file/clippers
	SPF lip balm	Tweezers
	Razor and shaving cream	Bug spray
	Shampoo and conditioner	Mini-laundry kit: travel
	Biodegradable soap/body wash	detergent, braided
	Toothbrush	clothesline, sink-stopper
	Toothpaste	
Miscellaneous	Travel pillow and blanket	Waterproof pocket camera
	Painkillers	Sleep sack
	Glasses	Pocket sewing kit
	Contact lenses & solution	Tripod
	Travel journal and pen	Travel alarm clock
	Books	Navigation - GPS/map/
	Sports sunglasses	compass
	Sun hat/cap/bandana	Hydration pack
	Quick-dry towel	Relevant activity equipment
	Water purifying bottle/pills	Refillable waterbottle
	Lighter/matches/flint	
	Waterproof bag	
	Multi-tool	
	Duct tape	
	Emergency whistle	

'HE WHO WOULD TRAVEL HAPPILY MUST TRAVEL LIGHT' ANTOINE DE ST-EXUPERY

Adventure

DESTINATION:

SPECIAL EVENTS:

DAYS: WEATHER:

	ESSENTIALS	ELECTRONICS
Basics	Passport (with visa if necessary)	Camera and charger
	Driving license	Mobile phone and charger
	Boarding passes/tickets	Tablet and charger
	Foreign cash	Headphones
	Credit/ATM cards	Plug adapters
	Guidebook	Torch/headtorch and batteries
	Maps/directions/itinerary	
	First aid kit	
	Travel insurance documents	
	Repeat and travel medication	
	Backpack/duffel w/outside pockets	
Clothes	Waterproof coat	Smart shoes
	Jumpers/fleeces	Trainers
	Convertible jacket	Water shoes
	Loose shirts	Waterproof watch
	Quick-drying tops	Hidden zipper belt
	T-shirts	Underwear/long underwear
	Cargo trousers	
	Convertible trousers	Sleepwear
	Loose trousers	Wool/thick socks
	Leggings	Warm hat/sun hat
	Shorts	Sunglasses
	Comfortable skirts	Insulating vests/tops
	Comfortable dresses	
	Walking boots	
	Hiking sandals	

'HE WHO WOULD TRAVEL HAPPILY MUST TRAVEL LIGHT' ANTOINE DE ST-EXUPERY

	DESTINATION:
	SPECIAL EVENTS:
	DAYS: WEATHER:

	ESSENTIALS	
Hygiene	Suncream and aftersun lotion	Make-up and remover
	Body lotion/moisturiser	Hairbrush/comb
	Insect repellent	Disposable wipes
	Deodorant	Sanitary products
	Perfume	Nail file/clippers
	SPF lip balm	Tweezers
	Razor and shaving cream	Bug spray
	Shampoo and conditioner	Mini-laundry kit: travel
	Biodegradable soap/body wash	detergent, braided
	Toothbrush	clothesline, sink-stopper
	Toothpaste	
Miscellaneous	Travel pillow and blanket	Waterproof pocket camera
	Painkillers	Sleep sack
	Glasses	Pocket sewing kit
	Contact lenses & solution	Tripod
	Travel journal and pen	Travel alarm clock
	Books	Navigation - GPS/map/
	Sports sunglasses	compass
	Sun hat/cap/bandana	Hydration pack
	Quick-dry towel	Relevant activity equipment
	Water purifying bottle/pills	Refillable waterbottle
	Lighter/matches/flint	
	Waterproof bag	
	Multi-tool	
	Duct tape	
	Emergency whistle	

'HE WHO WOULD TRAVEL HAPPILY MUST TRAVEL LIGHT' ANTOINE DE ST-EXUPERY

Adventure	DESTINATION: SPECIAL EVENTS: DAYS: WEATHER:

	ESSENTIALS	ELECTRONICS
Basics	Passport (with visa if necessary)	Camera and charger
	Driving license	Mobile phone and charger
	Boarding passes/tickets	Tablet and charger
	Foreign cash	Headphones
	Credit/ATM cards	Plug adapters
	Guidebook	Torch/headtorch and batteries
	Maps/directions/itinerary	
	First aid kit	
	Travel insurance documents	
	Repeat and travel medication	
	Backpack/duffel w/outside pockets	
Clothes	Waterproof coat	Smart shoes
	Jumpers/fleeces	Trainers
	Convertible jacket	Water shoes
	Loose shirts	Waterproof watch
	Quick-drying tops	Hidden zipper belt
	T-shirts	Underwear/long underwear
	Cargo trousers	Sleepwear
	Convertible trousers	Wool/thick socks
	Loose trousers	Warm hat/sun hat
	Leggings	Sunglasses
	Shorts	Insulating vests/tops
	Comfortable skirts	
	Comfortable dresses	
	Walking boots	
	Hiking sandals	

'HE WHO WOULD TRAVEL HAPPILY MUST TRAVEL LIGHT' ANTOINE DE ST-EXUPERY

	DESTINATION:
	SPECIAL EVENTS:
	DAYS: WEATHER:

	ESSENTIALS	
Hygiene	Suncream and aftersun	Make-up and remover
	lotion	Hairbrush/comb
	Body lotion/moisturiser	Disposable wipes
	Insect repellent	Sanitary products
	Deodorant	Nail file/clippers
	Perfume	Tweezers
	SPF lip balm	Bug spray
	Razor and shaving cream	Mini-laundry kit: travel
	Shampoo and conditioner	detergent, braided
	Biodegradable soap/body	clothesline, sink-stopper
	wash	
	Toothbrush	
	Toothpaste	
Miscellaneous	Travel pillow and blanket	Waterproof pocket camera
	Painkillers	Sleep sack
	Glasses	Pocket sewing kit
	Contact lenses & solution	Tripod
	Travel journal and pen	Travel alarm clock
	Books	Navigation - GPS/map/
	Sports sunglasses	compass
	Sun hat/cap/bandana	Hydration pack
	Quick-dry towel	Relevant activity equipment
	Water purifying bottle/pills	Refillable waterbottle
	Lighter/matches/flint	
	Waterproof bag	
	Multi-tool	
	Duct tape	
	Emergency whistle	

'HE WHO WOULD TRAVEL HAPPILY MUST TRAVEL LIGHT' ANTOINE DE ST-EXUPERY

Adventure

	ESSENTIALS	ELECTRONICS
Basics	Passport (with visa if necessary)	Camera and charger
	Driving license	Mobile phone and charger
	Boarding passes/tickets	Tablet and charger
	Foreign cash	Headphones
	Credit/ATM cards	Plug adapters
	Guidebook	Torch/headtorch and batteries
	Maps/directions/itinerary	
	First aid kit	
	Travel insurance documents	
	Repeat and travel medication	
	Backpack/duffel w/outside pockets	
Clothes	Waterproof coat	Smart shoes
	Jumpers/fleeces	Trainers
	Convertible jacket	Water shoes
	Loose shirts	Waterproof watch
	Quick-drying tops	Hidden zipper belt
	T-shirts	Underwear/long underwear
	Cargo trousers	
	Convertible trousers	Sleepwear
	Loose trousers	Wool/thick socks
	Leggings	Warm hat/sun hat
	Shorts	Sunglasses
	Comfortable skirts	Insulating vests/tops
	Comfortable dresses	
	Walking boots	
	Hiking sandals	

'HE WHO WOULD TRAVEL HAPPILY MUST TRAVEL LIGHT' ANTOINE DE ST-EXUPERY

	DESTINATION:
	SPECIAL EVENTS:
	DAYS: WEATHER:

	ESSENTIALS	
Hygiene	Suncream and aftersun lotion	Make-up and remover
	Body lotion/moisturiser	Hairbrush/comb
	Insect repellent	Disposable wipes
	Deodorant	Sanitary products
	Perfume	Nail file/clippers
	SPF lip balm	Tweezers
	Razor and shaving cream	Bug spray
	Shampoo and conditioner	Mini-laundry kit: travel
	Biodegradable soap/body wash	detergent, braided
	Toothbrush	clothesline, sink-stopper
	Toothpaste	
Miscellaneous	Travel pillow and blanket	Waterproof pocket camera
	Painkillers	Sleep sack
	Glasses	Pocket sewing kit
	Contact lenses & solution	Tripod
	Travel journal and pen	Travel alarm clock
	Books	Navigation - GPS/map/
	Sports sunglasses	compass
	Sun hat/cap/bandana	Hydration pack
	Quick-dry towel	Relevant activity equipment
	Water purifying bottle/pills	Refillable waterbottle
	Lighter/matches/flint	
	Waterproof bag	
	Multi-tool	
	Duct tape	
	Emergency whistle	

'HE WHO WOULD TRAVEL HAPPILY MUST TRAVEL LIGHT' ANTOINE DE ST-EXUPERY

Adventure

DESTINATION:
SPECIAL EVENTS:
DAYS: WEATHER:

	ESSENTIALS	ELECTRONICS
Basics	Passport (with visa if necessary)	Camera and charger
	Driving license	Mobile phone and charger
	Boarding passes/tickets	Tablet and charger
	Foreign cash	Headphones
	Credit/ATM cards	Plug adapters
	Guidebook	Torch/headtorch and batteries
	Maps/directions/itinerary	
	First aid kit	
	Travel insurance documents	
	Repeat and travel medication	
	Backpack/duffel w/outside pockets	
Clothes	Waterproof coat	Smart shoes
	Jumpers/fleeces	Trainers
	Convertible jacket	Water shoes
	Loose shirts	Waterproof watch
	Quick-drying tops	Hidden zipper belt
	T-shirts	Underwear/long under-wear
	Cargo trousers	Sleepwear
	Convertible trousers	Wool/thick socks
	Loose trousers	Warm hat/sun hat
	Leggings	Sunglasses
	Shorts	Insulating vests/tops
	Comfortable skirts	
	Comfortable dresses	
	Walking boots	
	Hiking sandals	

'HE WHO WOULD TRAVEL HAPPILY MUST TRAVEL LIGHT' ANTOINE DE ST-EXUPERY

ESSENTIALS		
	Suncream and aftersun	Make-up and remover
	lotion	Hairbrush/comb
	Body lotion/moisturiser	Disposable wipes
Hygiene	Insect repellent	Sanitary products
	Deodorant	Nail file/clippers
	Perfume	Tweezers
	SPF lip balm	Bug spray
	Razor and shaving cream	Mini-laundry kit: travel
	Shampoo and conditioner	detergent, braided
	Biodegradable soap/body	clothesline, sink-stopper
	wash	
	Toothbrush	
	Toothpaste	
	Travel pillow and blanket	Waterproof pocket camera
	Painkillers	Sleep sack
	Glasses	Pocket sewing kit
	Contact lenses & solution	Tripod
	Travel journal and pen	Travel alarm clock
Miscellaneous	Books	Navigation - GPS/map/
	Sports sunglasses	compass
	Sun hat/cap/bandana	Hydration pack
	Quick-dry towel	Relevant activity equipment
	Water purifying bottle/pills	Refillable waterbottle
	Lighter/matches/flint	
	Waterproof bag	
	Multi-tool	
	Duct tape	
	Emergency whistle	

'HE WHO WOULD TRAVEL HAPPILY MUST TRAVEL LIGHT' ANTOINE DE ST-EXUPERY

Adventure		DESTINATION:
		SPECIAL EVENTS:
		DAYS: WEATHER:

	ESSENTIALS	ELECTRONICS
Basics	Passport (with visa if necessary)	Camera and charger
	Driving license	Mobile phone and charger
	Boarding passes/tickets	Tablet and charger
	Foreign cash	Headphones
	Credit/ATM cards	Plug adapters
	Guidebook	Torch/headtorch and batteries
	Maps/directions/itinerary	
	First aid kit	
	Travel insurance documents	
	Repeat and travel medication	
	Backpack/duffel w/outside pockets	
Clothes	Waterproof coat	Smart shoes
	Jumpers/fleeces	Trainers
	Convertible jacket	Water shoes
	Loose shirts	Waterproof watch
	Quick-drying tops	Hidden zipper belt
	T-shirts	Underwear/long underwear
	Cargo trousers	Sleepwear
	Convertible trousers	Wool/thick socks
	Loose trousers	Warm hat/sun hat
	Leggings	Sunglasses
	Shorts	Insulating vests/tops
	Comfortable skirts	
	Comfortable dresses	
	Walking boots	
	Hiking sandals	

'HE WHO WOULD TRAVEL HAPPILY MUST TRAVEL LIGHT' ANTOINE DE ST-EXUPERY

	DESTINATION:
	SPECIAL EVENTS:
	DAYS: WEATHER:

	ESSENTIALS	
Hygiene	Suncream and aftersun lotion	Make-up and remover
	Body lotion/moisturiser	Hairbrush/comb
	Insect repellent	Disposable wipes
	Deodorant	Sanitary products
	Perfume	Nail file/clippers
	SPF lip balm	Tweezers
	Razor and shaving cream	Bug spray
	Shampoo and conditioner	Mini-laundry kit: travel
	Biodegradable soap/body wash	detergent, braided clothesline, sink-stopper
	Toothbrush	
	Toothpaste	
Miscellaneous	Travel pillow and blanket	Waterproof pocket camera
	Painkillers	Sleep sack
	Glasses	Pocket sewing kit
	Contact lenses & solution	Tripod
	Travel journal and pen	Travel alarm clock
	Books	Navigation - GPS/map/
	Sports sunglasses	compass
	Sun hat/cap/bandana	Hydration pack
	Quick-dry towel	Relevant activity equipment
	Water purifying bottle/pills	Refillable waterbottle
	Lighter/matches/flint	
	Waterproof bag	
	Multi-tool	
	Duct tape	
	Emergency whistle	

'HE WHO WOULD TRAVEL HAPPILY MUST TRAVEL LIGHT' ANTOINE DE ST-EXUPERY

	DESTINATION:
	SPECIAL EVENTS:
Family	DAYS: WEATHER:

	ESSENTIALS	ELECTRONICS
Basics	Passport (with visa if necessary)	Camera and charger
	Driving license	Mobile phone and charger
	Boarding passes/tickets	Tablet and charger
	Foreign cash	Headphones
	Credit/ATM cards	Plug adapters
	Maps/itinerary/car hire documents	Kids TV/films/games
	Guidebook	
	Travel insurance documents	
	Childrens' medication	
	Repeat and travel medication	
	Proof of relationship papers	
Clothes	Jackets/coats	Sandals
	Waterproof coats	Smart shoes
	Jumpers	Flip-flops
	Casual shirts	Trainers/leisure shoes
	Vest tops	Water booties
	T-shirts	Belts
	Jeans	Socks
	Smart trousers	Underwear
	Loose trousers	Tights
	Leggings	Sleepwear
	Shorts	Jewellery
	Skirts	Swimsuit
	Dungarees	Sarong/shawl
	Day dresses	Sun hats
	Evening dresses	

'HE WHO WOULD TRAVEL HAPPILY MUST TRAVEL LIGHT' ANTOINE DE ST-EXUPERY

DESTINATION:

SPECIAL EVENTS:

DAYS: WEATHER:

ESSENTIALS	
Suncream and aftersun	Disposable wipes
lotion for all	Sanitary products
Body lotion/moisturiser	Nail file/clippers
Insect repellent	Tweezers
Deodorant	Bug spray
Perfume	Baby wipes
SPF lip balm	Nappies, nappy cream,
Razor and shaving cream	wipes
Shampoo and conditioner	Reusable swim nappies
for all	Plasters
Soap/body wash	Toilet roll
Toothbrush	Talcum powder
Toothpaste	Washing tablets
Make-up and remover	First-aid kit
Hairbrush/comb	
Hair products	

Hygiene

Travel pillow and blanket	Snacks
Painkillers	Foldable pram
Glasses	Travel board games
Contact lenses & solution	Playing cards
Travel journal and pen	Drawing supplies
Books	Sippy cups/bottles
Sunglasses	Milk and baby food
Towels	Dummy and teething gel
Backpack/hands-free bag	Changing mat
Refillable bottles	Picnic box/bag
Kids travel tent	Sling
Comforter/favourite toy	Buggy
Child-size suitcase/backpack	

Miscellaneous

'HE WHO WOULD TRAVEL HAPPILY MUST TRAVEL LIGHT' ANTOINE DE ST-EXUPERY

Family

Basics

ESSENTIALS	ELECTRONICS
Passport (with visa if necessary)	Camera and charger
Driving license	Mobile phone and charger
Boarding passes/tickets	Tablet and charger
Foreign cash	Headphones
Credit/ATM cards	Plug adapters
Maps/itinerary/car hire documents	Kids TV/films/games
Guidebook	
Travel insurance documents	
Childrens' medication	
Repeat and travel medication	
Proof of relationship papers	

Clothes

Jackets/coats	Sandals
Waterproof coats	Smart shoes
Jumpers	Flip-flops
Casual shirts	Trainers/leisure shoes
Vest tops	Water booties
T-shirts	Belts
Jeans	Socks
Smart trousers	Underwear
Loose trousers	Tights
Leggings	Sleepwear
Shorts	Jewellery
Skirts	Swimsuit
Dungarees	Sarong/shawl
Day dresses	Sun hats
Evening dresses	

'HE WHO WOULD TRAVEL HAPPILY MUST TRAVEL LIGHT' ANTOINE DE ST-EXUPERY

| DESTINATION: |
| SPECIAL EVENTS: |
| DAYS: WEATHER: |

	ESSENTIALS	
Hygiene	Suncream and aftersun lotion for all	Disposable wipes
	Body lotion/moisturiser	Sanitary products
	Insect repellent	Nail file/clippers
	Deodorant	Tweezers
	Perfume	Bug spray
	SPF lip balm	Baby wipes
	Razor and shaving cream	Nappies, nappy cream, wipes
	Shampoo and conditioner for all	Reusable swim nappies
	Soap/body wash	Plasters
	Toothbrush	Toilet roll
	Toothpaste	Talcum powder
	Make-up and remover	Washing tablets
	Hairbrush/comb	First-aid kit
	Hair products	
Miscellaneous	Travel pillow and blanket	Snacks
	Painkillers	Foldable pram
	Glasses	Travel board games
	Contact lenses & solution	Playing cards
	Travel journal and pen	Drawing supplies
	Books	Sippy cups/bottles
	Sunglasses	Milk and baby food
	Towels	Dummy and teething gel
	Backpack/hands-free bag	Changing mat
	Refillable bottles	Picnic box/bag
	Kids travel tent	Sling
	Comforter/favourite toy	Buggy
	Child-size suitcase/backpack	

'HE WHO WOULD TRAVEL HAPPILY MUST TRAVEL LIGHT' ANTOINE DE ST-EXUPERY

Family

DESTINATION:

SPECIAL EVENTS:

DAYS: WEATHER:

Basics

ESSENTIALS	ELECTRONICS
Passport (with visa if necessary)	Camera and charger
Driving license	Mobile phone and charger
Boarding passes/tickets	Tablet and charger
Foreign cash	Headphones
Credit/ATM cards	Plug adapters
Maps/itinerary/car hire documents	Kids TV/films/games
Guidebook	
Travel insurance documents	
Childrens' medication	
Repeat and travel medication	
Proof of relationship papers	

Clothes

Jackets/coats	Sandals
Waterproof coats	Smart shoes
Jumpers	Flip-flops
Casual shirts	Trainers/leisure shoes
Vest tops	Water booties
T-shirts	Belts
Jeans	Socks
Smart trousers	Underwear
Loose trousers	Tights
Leggings	Sleepwear
Shorts	Jewellery
Skirts	Swimsuit
Dungarees	Sarong/shawl
Day dresses	Sun hats
Evening dresses	

'HE WHO WOULD TRAVEL HAPPILY MUST TRAVEL LIGHT' ANTOINE DE ST-EXUPERY

		DESTINATION:
		SPECIAL EVENTS:
		DAYS: WEATHER:

	ESSENTIALS	
Hygiene	Suncream and aftersun	Disposable wipes
	lotion for all	Sanitary products
	Body lotion/moisturiser	Nail file/clippers
	Insect repellent	Tweezers
	Deodorant	Bug spray
	Perfume	Baby wipes
	SPF lip balm	Nappies, nappy cream,
	Razor and shaving cream	wipes
	Shampoo and conditioner	Reusable swim nappies
	for all	Plasters
	Soap/body wash	Toilet roll
	Toothbrush	Talcum powder
	Toothpaste	Washing tablets
	Make-up and remover	First-aid kit
	Hairbrush/comb	
	Hair products	
Miscellaneous	Travel pillow and blanket	Snacks
	Painkillers	Foldable pram
	Glasses	Travel board games
	Contact lenses & solution	Playing cards
	Travel journal and pen	Drawing supplies
	Books	Sippy cups/bottles
	Sunglasses	Milk and baby food
	Towels	Dummy and teething gel
	Backpack/hands-free bag	Changing mat
	Refillable bottles	Picnic box/bag
	Kids travel tent	Sling
	Comforter/favourite toy	Buggy
	Child-size suitcase/backpack	

'HE WHO WOULD TRAVEL HAPPILY MUST TRAVEL LIGHT' ANTOINE DE ST-EXUPERY

Family

	ESSENTIALS	ELECTRONICS
Basics	Passport (with visa if necessary)	Camera and charger
	Driving license	Mobile phone and charger
	Boarding passes/tickets	Tablet and charger
	Foreign cash	Headphones
	Credit/ATM cards	Plug adapters
	Maps/itinerary/car hire documents	Kids TV/films/games
	Guidebook	
	Travel insurance documents	
	Childrens' medication	
	Repeat and travel medication	
	Proof of relationship papers	
Clothes	Jackets/coats	Sandals
	Waterproof coats	Smart shoes
	Jumpers	Flip-flops
	Casual shirts	Trainers/leisure shoes
	Vest tops	Water booties
	T-shirts	Belts
	Jeans	Socks
	Smart trousers	Underwear
	Loose trousers	Tights
	Leggings	Sleepwear
	Shorts	Jewellery
	Skirts	Swimsuit
	Dungarees	Sarong/shawl
	Day dresses	Sun hats
	Evening dresses	

'HE WHO WOULD TRAVEL HAPPILY MUST TRAVEL LIGHT' ANTOINE DE ST-EXUPERY

	ESSENTIALS	
Hygiene	Suncream and aftersun lotion for all	Disposable wipes
	Body lotion/moisturiser	Sanitary products
	Insect repellent	Nail file/clippers
	Deodorant	Tweezers
	Perfume	Bug spray
	SPF lip balm	Baby wipes
	Razor and shaving cream	Nappies, nappy cream, wipes
	Shampoo and conditioner for all	Reusable swim nappies
	Soap/body wash	Plasters
	Toothbrush	Toilet roll
	Toothpaste	Talcum powder
	Make-up and remover	Washing tablets
	Hairbrush/comb	First-aid kit
	Hair products	
Miscellaneous	Travel pillow and blanket	Snacks
	Painkillers	Foldable pram
	Glasses	Travel board games
	Contact lenses & solution	Playing cards
	Travel journal and pen	Drawing supplies
	Books	Sippy cups/bottles
	Sunglasses	Milk and baby food
	Towels	Dummy and teething gel
	Backpack/hands-free bag	Changing mat
	Refillable bottles	Picnic box/bag
	Kids travel tent	Sling
	Comforter/favourite toy	Buggy
	Child-size suitcase/backpack	

'HE WHO WOULD TRAVEL HAPPILY MUST TRAVEL LIGHT' ANTOINE DE ST-EXUPERY

	Family	DESTINATION: SPECIAL EVENTS: DAYS: WEATHER:

	ESSENTIALS	ELECTRONICS
Basics	Passport (with visa if necessary)	Camera and charger
	Driving license	Mobile phone and charger
	Boarding passes/tickets	Tablet and charger
	Foreign cash	Headphones
	Credit/ATM cards	Plug adapters
	Maps/itinerary/car hire documents	Kids TV/films/games
	Guidebook	
	Travel insurance documents	
	Childrens' medication	
	Repeat and travel medication	
	Proof of relationship papers	
Clothes	Jackets/coats	Sandals
	Waterproof coats	Smart shoes
	Jumpers	Flip-flops
	Casual shirts	Trainers/leisure shoes
	Vest tops	Water booties
	T-shirts	Belts
	Jeans	Socks
	Smart trousers	Underwear
	Loose trousers	Tights
	Leggings	Sleepwear
	Shorts	Jewellery
	Skirts	Swimsuit
	Dungarees	Sarong/shawl
	Day dresses	Sun hats
	Evening dresses	

'HE WHO WOULD TRAVEL HAPPILY MUST TRAVEL LIGHT' ANTOINE DE ST-EXUPERY

DESTINATION:

SPECIAL EVENTS:

DAYS: WEATHER:

	ESSENTIALS		
Hygiene	Suncream and aftersun lotion for all		Disposable wipes
	Body lotion/moisturiser		Sanitary products
	Insect repellent		Nail file/clippers
	Deodorant		Tweezers
	Perfume		Bug spray
	SPF lip balm		Baby wipes
	Razor and shaving cream		Nappies, nappy cream, wipes
	Shampoo and conditioner for all		Reusable swim nappies
	Soap/body wash		Plasters
	Toothbrush		Toilet roll
	Toothpaste		Talcum powder
	Make-up and remover		Washing tablets
	Hairbrush/comb		First-aid kit
	Hair products		
Miscellaneous	Travel pillow and blanket		Snacks
	Painkillers		Foldable pram
	Glasses		Travel board games
	Contact lenses & solution		Playing cards
	Travel journal and pen		Drawing supplies
	Books		Sippy cups/bottles
	Sunglasses		Milk and baby food
	Towels		Dummy and teething gel
	Backpack/hands-free bag		Changing mat
	Refillable bottles		Picnic box/bag
	Kids travel tent		Sling
	Comforter/favourite toy		Buggy
	Child-size suitcase/backpack		

'HE WHO WOULD TRAVEL HAPPILY MUST TRAVEL LIGHT' ANTOINE DE ST-EXUPERY

Family	SPECIAL EVENTS:	
	DAYS: WEATHER:	

	ESSENTIALS	ELECTRONICS
Basics	Passport (with visa if necessary)	Camera and charger
	Driving license	Mobile phone and charger
	Boarding passes/tickets	Tablet and charger
	Foreign cash	Headphones
	Credit/ATM cards	Plug adapters
	Maps/itinerary/car hire documents	Kids TV/films/games
	Guidebook	
	Travel insurance documents	
	Childrens' medication	
	Repeat and travel medication	
	Proof of relationship papers	
Clothes	Jackets/coats	Sandals
	Waterproof coats	Smart shoes
	Jumpers	Flip-flops
	Casual shirts	Trainers/leisure shoes
	Vest tops	Water booties
	T-shirts	Belts
	Jeans	Socks
	Smart trousers	Underwear
	Loose trousers	Tights
	Leggings	Sleepwear
	Shorts	Jewellery
	Skirts	Swimsuit
	Dungarees	Sarong/shawl
	Day dresses	Sun hats
	Evening dresses	

'HE WHO WOULD TRAVEL HAPPILY MUST TRAVEL LIGHT' ANTOINE DE ST-EXUPERY

		DESTINATION:
		SPECIAL EVENTS:
		DAYS: WEATHER:

	ESSENTIALS	
Hygiene	Suncream and aftersun lotion for all	Disposable wipes
	Body lotion/moisturiser	Sanitary products
	Insect repellent	Nail file/clippers
	Deodorant	Tweezers
	Perfume	Bug spray
	SPF lip balm	Baby wipes
	Razor and shaving cream	Nappies, nappy cream, wipes
	Shampoo and conditioner for all	Reusable swim nappies
	Soap/body wash	Plasters
	Toothbrush	Toilet roll
	Toothpaste	Talcum powder
	Make-up and remover	Washing tablets
	Hairbrush/comb	First-aid kit
	Hair products	
Miscellaneous	Travel pillow and blanket	Snacks
	Painkillers	Foldable pram
	Glasses	Travel board games
	Contact lenses & solution	Playing cards
	Travel journal and pen	Drawing supplies
	Books	Sippy cups/bottles
	Sunglasses	Milk and baby food
	Towels	Dummy and teething gel
	Backpack/hands-free bag	Changing mat
	Refillable bottles	Picnic box/bag
	Kids travel tent	Sling
	Comforter/favourite toy	Buggy
	Child-size suitcase/backpack	

'HE WHO WOULD TRAVEL HAPPILY MUST TRAVEL LIGHT' ANTOINE DE ST-EXUPERY

Family

	ESSENTIALS	ELECTRONICS
Basics	Passport (with visa if necessary)	Camera and charger
	Driving license	Mobile phone and charger
	Boarding passes/tickets	Tablet and charger
	Foreign cash	Headphones
	Credit/ATM cards	Plug adapters
	Maps/itinerary/car hire documents	Kids TV/films/games
	Guidebook	
	Travel insurance documents	
	Childrens' medication	
	Repeat and travel medication	
	Proof of relationship papers	
Clothes	Jackets/coats	Sandals
	Waterproof coats	Smart shoes
	Jumpers	Flip-flops
	Casual shirts	Trainers/leisure shoes
	Vest tops	Water booties
	T-shirts	Belts
	Jeans	Socks
	Smart trousers	Underwear
	Loose trousers	Tights
	Leggings	Sleepwear
	Shorts	Jewellery
	Skirts	Swimsuit
	Dungarees	Sarong/shawl
	Day dresses	Sun hats
	Evening dresses	

'HE WHO WOULD TRAVEL HAPPILY MUST TRAVEL LIGHT' ANTOINE DE ST-EXUPERY

| | DESTINATION: |
| SPECIAL EVENTS: |
| DAYS: WEATHER: |

	ESSENTIALS	
Hygiene	Suncream and aftersun lotion for all	Disposable wipes
	Body lotion/moisturiser	Sanitary products
	Insect repellent	Nail file/clippers
	Deodorant	Tweezers
	Perfume	Bug spray
	SPF lip balm	Baby wipes
	Razor and shaving cream	Nappies, nappy cream,
	Shampoo and conditioner for all	wipes
		Reusable swim nappies
	Soap/body wash	Plasters
	Toothbrush	Toilet roll
	Toothpaste	Talcum powder
	Make-up and remover	Washing tablets
	Hairbrush/comb	First-aid kit
	Hair products	
Miscellaneous	Travel pillow and blanket	Snacks
	Painkillers	Foldable pram
	Glasses	Travel board games
	Contact lenses & solution	Playing cards
	Travel journal and pen	Drawing supplies
	Books	Sippy cups/bottles
	Sunglasses	Milk and baby food
	Towels	Dummy and teething gel
	Backpack/hands-free bag	Changing mat
	Refillable bottles	Picnic box/bag
	Kids travel tent	Sling
	Comforter/favourite toy	Buggy
	Child-size suitcase/backpack	

'HE WHO WOULD TRAVEL HAPPILY MUST TRAVEL LIGHT' ANTOINE DE ST-EXUPERY

Family

Basics

ESSENTIALS	ELECTRONICS
Passport (with visa if necessary)	Camera and charger
Driving license	Mobile phone and charger
Boarding passes/tickets	Tablet and charger
Foreign cash	Headphones
Credit/ATM cards	Plug adapters
Maps/itinerary/car hire documents	Kids TV/films/games
Guidebook	
Travel insurance documents	
Childrens' medication	
Repeat and travel medication	
Proof of relationship papers	

Clothes

Jackets/coats	Sandals
Waterproof coats	Smart shoes
Jumpers	Flip-flops
Casual shirts	Trainers/leisure shoes
Vest tops	Water booties
T-shirts	Belts
Jeans	Socks
Smart trousers	Underwear
Loose trousers	Tights
Leggings	Sleepwear
Shorts	Jewellery
Skirts	Swimsuit
Dungarees	Sarong/shawl
Day dresses	Sun hats
Evening dresses	

'HE WHO WOULD TRAVEL HAPPILY MUST TRAVEL LIGHT' ANTOINE DE ST-EXUPERY

	ESSENTIALS	
Hygiene	Suncream and aftersun	Disposable wipes
	lotion for all	Sanitary products
	Body lotion/moisturiser	Nail file/clippers
	Insect repellent	Tweezers
	Deodorant	Bug spray
	Perfume	Baby wipes
	SPF lip balm	Nappies, nappy cream,
	Razor and shaving cream	wipes
	Shampoo and conditioner	Reusable swim nappies
	for all	Plasters
	Soap/body wash	Toilet roll
	Toothbrush	Talcum powder
	Toothpaste	Washing tablets
	Make-up and remover	First-aid kit
	Hairbrush/comb	
	Hair products	
Miscellaneous	Travel pillow and blanket	Snacks
	Painkillers	Foldable pram
	Glasses	Travel board games
	Contact lenses & solution	Playing cards
	Travel journal and pen	Drawing supplies
	Books	Sippy cups/bottles
	Sunglasses	Milk and baby food
	Towels	Dummy and teething gel
	Backpack/hands-free bag	Changing mat
	Refillable bottles	Picnic box/bag
	Kids travel tent	Sling
	Comforter/favourite toy	Buggy
	Child-size suitcase/backpack	

'HE WHO WOULD TRAVEL HAPPILY MUST TRAVEL LIGHT' ANTOINE DE ST-EXUPERY

| | **Family** | SPECIAL EVENTS: |
| | | DAYS: WEATHER: |

	ESSENTIALS	ELECTRONICS
Basics	Passport (with visa if necessary)	Camera and charger
	Driving license	Mobile phone and charger
	Boarding passes/tickets	Tablet and charger
	Foreign cash	Headphones
	Credit/ATM cards	Plug adapters
	Maps/itinerary/car hire documents	Kids TV/films/games
	Guidebook	
	Travel insurance documents	
	Childrens' medication	
	Repeat and travel medication	
	Proof of relationship papers	
Clothes	Jackets/coats	Sandals
	Waterproof coats	Smart shoes
	Jumpers	Flip-flops
	Casual shirts	Trainers/leisure shoes
	Vest tops	Water booties
	T-shirts	Belts
	Jeans	Socks
	Smart trousers	Underwear
	Loose trousers	Tights
	Leggings	Sleepwear
	Shorts	Jewellery
	Skirts	Swimsuit
	Dungarees	Sarong/shawl
	Day dresses	Sun hats
	Evening dresses	

'HE WHO WOULD TRAVEL HAPPILY MUST TRAVEL LIGHT' ANTOINE DE ST-EXUPERY

	ESSENTIALS	
Hygiene	Suncream and aftersun	Disposable wipes
	lotion for all	Sanitary products
	Body lotion/moisturiser	Nail file/clippers
	Insect repellent	Tweezers
	Deodorant	Bug spray
	Perfume	Baby wipes
	SPF lip balm	Nappies, nappy cream,
	Razor and shaving cream	wipes
	Shampoo and conditioner	Reusable swim nappies
	for all	Plasters
	Soap/body wash	Toilet roll
	Toothbrush	Talcum powder
	Toothpaste	Washing tablets
	Make-up and remover	First-aid kit
	Hairbrush/comb	
	Hair products	
Miscellaneous	Travel pillow and blanket	Snacks
	Painkillers	Foldable pram
	Glasses	Travel board games
	Contact lenses & solution	Playing cards
	Travel journal and pen	Drawing supplies
	Books	Sippy cups/bottles
	Sunglasses	Milk and baby food
	Towels	Dummy and teething gel
	Backpack/hands-free bag	Changing mat
	Refillable bottles	Picnic box/bag
	Kids travel tent	Sling
	Comforter/favourite toy	Buggy
	Child-size suitcase/backpack	

'HE WHO WOULD TRAVEL HAPPILY MUST TRAVEL LIGHT' ANTOINE DE ST-EXUPERY

Backpacking

ESSENTIALS	ELECTRONICS
Passport	Camera and charger
Boarding passes	Mobile phone and
Foreign cash	charger
Credit/ATM cards	Tablet and charger
Maps/directions/itinerary	Headphones
Guidebook material	Plug adapters
First aid kit	Torch/headtorch and
Travel insurance documents	batteries
Repeat and travel medication	Waterproof pocket
Folder for all documents	camera
Large backpack	Back-up hard drive
Small combination lock	

Basics

Light jacket	Belt
Waterproof coat	Thin socks
Light jumpers	Underwear
Thin hoodie	Sleepwear
Casual shirts	Sun hat/cap
Vest tops	Swimsuit
T-shirts	Sarong/shawl
Loose trousers	Hidden zipper belt
Leggings	
Shorts	
Skirts	
Dresses	
Sandals	
Flip-flops	
Trainers/comfortable shoes	

Clothes

'HE WHO WOULD TRAVEL HAPPILY MUST TRAVEL LIGHT' ANTOINE DE ST-EXUPERY

	ESSENTIALS	
Hygiene	Suncream and aftersun	Hair products
	lotion	Disposable wipes
	Body lotion/moisturiser	Sanitary products
	Insect repellent	Nail file/clippers
	Deodorant	Tweezers
	Perfume	Bug spray
	SPF lip balm	Laundry kit: travel deter-
	Razor and shaving cream	gent, braided clothes-
	Shampoo and conditioner	line, sink-stopper
	Soap/body wash	Hand sanitizer
	Toothbrush	Dental floss
	Toothpaste	Small tubes for liquids
	Make-up and remover	Tissues
	Hairbrush/comb	
Miscellaneous	Painkillers	Playing cards
	Glasses	Pocket sewing kit
	Contact lenses & solution	Sleeping bag (optional)
	Travel journal and pen	Portable stove
	Books	Cutlery
	Sunglasses	Bowl/cup
	Waterproof watch	
	Beach towel/quick-dry towel	
	Waterproof bag	
	Water purifying bottle	
	Sleep sack	
	Earplugs	
	Refillable bottles	
	Travel neck pillow	

'HE WHO WOULD TRAVEL HAPPILY MUST TRAVEL LIGHT' ANTOINE DE ST-EXUPERY

Backpacking

	ESSENTIALS	ELECTRONICS
Basics	Passport	Camera and charger
	Boarding passes	Mobile phone and
	Foreign cash	charger
	Credit/ATM cards	Tablet and charger
	Maps/directions/itinerary	Headphones
	Guidebook material	Plug adapters
	First aid kit	Torch/headtorch and
	Travel insurance documents	batteries
	Repeat and travel medication	Waterproof pocket
	Folder for all documents	camera
	Large backpack	Back-up hard drive
	Small combination lock	
Clothes	Light jacket	Belt
	Waterproof coat	Thin socks
	Light jumpers	Underwear
	Thin hoodie	Sleepwear
	Casual shirts	Sun hat/cap
	Vest tops	Swimsuit
	T-shirts	Sarong/shawl
	Loose trousers	Hidden zipper belt
	Leggings	
	Shorts	
	Skirts	
	Dresses	
	Sandals	
	Flip-flops	
	Trainers/comfortable shoes	

'HE WHO WOULD TRAVEL HAPPILY MUST TRAVEL LIGHT' ANTOINE DE ST-EXUPERY

	ESSENTIALS	
Hygiene	Suncream and aftersun	Hair products
	lotion	Disposable wipes
	Body lotion/moisturiser	Sanitary products
	Insect repellent	Nail file/clippers
	Deodorant	Tweezers
	Perfume	Bug spray
	SPF lip balm	Laundry kit: travel deter-
	Razor and shaving cream	gent, braided clothes-
	Shampoo and conditioner	line, sink-stopper
	Soap/body wash	Hand sanitizer
	Toothbrush	Dental floss
	Toothpaste	Small tubes for liquids
	Make-up and remover	Tissues
	Hairbrush/comb	
Miscellaneous	Painkillers	Playing cards
	Glasses	Pocket sewing kit
	Contact lenses & solution	Sleeping bag (optional)
	Travel journal and pen	Portable stove
	Books	Cutlery
	Sunglasses	Bowl/cup
	Waterproof watch	
	Beach towel/quick-dry towel	
	Waterproof bag	
	Water purifying bottle	
	Sleep sack	
	Earplugs	
	Refillable bottles	
	Travel neck pillow	

'HE WHO WOULD TRAVEL HAPPILY MUST TRAVEL LIGHT' ANTOINE DE ST-EXUPERY

Backpacking

	ESSENTIALS	ELECTRONICS
Basics	Passport	Camera and charger
	Boarding passes	Mobile phone and
	Foreign cash	charger
	Credit/ATM cards	Tablet and charger
	Maps/directions/itinerary	Headphones
	Guidebook material	Plug adapters
	First aid kit	Torch/headtorch and
	Travel insurance documents	batteries
	Repeat and travel medication	Waterproof pocket
	Folder for all documents	camera
	Large backpack	Back-up hard drive
	Small combination lock	
Clothes	Light jacket	Belt
	Waterproof coat	Thin socks
	Light jumpers	Underwear
	Thin hoodie	Sleepwear
	Casual shirts	Sun hat/cap
	Vest tops	Swimsuit
	T-shirts	Sarong/shawl
	Loose trousers	Hidden zipper belt
	Leggings	
	Shorts	
	Skirts	
	Dresses	
	Sandals	
	Flip-flops	
	Trainers/comfortable shoes	

'HE WHO WOULD TRAVEL HAPPILY MUST TRAVEL LIGHT' ANTOINE DE ST-EXUPERY

ESSENTIALS	
Hygiene	
Suncream and aftersun lotion	Hair products
Body lotion/moisturiser	Disposable wipes
Insect repellent	Sanitary products
Deodorant	Nail file/clippers
Perfume	Tweezers
SPF lip balm	Bug spray
Razor and shaving cream	Laundry kit: travel detergent, braided clothes-line, sink-stopper
Shampoo and conditioner	
Soap/body wash	Hand sanitizer
Toothbrush	Dental floss
Toothpaste	Small tubes for liquids
Make-up and remover	Tissues
Hairbrush/comb	
Miscellaneous	
Painkillers	Playing cards
Glasses	Pocket sewing kit
Contact lenses & solution	Sleeping bag (optional)
Travel journal and pen	Portable stove
Books	Cutlery
Sunglasses	Bowl/cup
Waterproof watch	
Beach towel/quick-dry towel	
Waterproof bag	
Water purifying bottle	
Sleep sack	
Earplugs	
Refillable bottles	
Travel neck pillow	

'HE WHO WOULD TRAVEL HAPPILY MUST TRAVEL LIGHT' ANTOINE DE ST-EXUPERY

Backpacking

Basics

ESSENTIALS	ELECTRONICS
Passport	Camera and charger
Boarding passes	Mobile phone and
Foreign cash	charger
Credit/ATM cards	Tablet and charger
Maps/directions/itinerary	Headphones
Guidebook material	Plug adapters
First aid kit	Torch/headtorch and
Travel insurance documents	batteries
Repeat and travel medication	Waterproof pocket
Folder for all documents	camera
Large backpack	Back-up hard drive
Small combination lock	

Clothes

Light jacket	Belt
Waterproof coat	Thin socks
Light jumpers	Underwear
Thin hoodie	Sleepwear
Casual shirts	Sun hat/cap
Vest tops	Swimsuit
T-shirts	Sarong/shawl
Loose trousers	Hidden zipper belt
Leggings	
Shorts	
Skirts	
Dresses	
Sandals	
Flip-flops	
Trainers/comfortable shoes	

'HE WHO WOULD TRAVEL HAPPILY MUST TRAVEL LIGHT' ANTOINE DE ST-EXUPERY

ESSENTIALS	
Suncream and aftersun	Hair products
lotion	Disposable wipes
Body lotion/moisturiser	Sanitary products
Insect repellent	Nail file/clippers
Deodorant	Tweezers
Perfume	Bug spray
SPF lip balm	Laundry kit: travel deter-
Razor and shaving cream	gent, braided clothes-
Shampoo and conditioner	line, sink-stopper
Soap/body wash	Hand sanitizer
Toothbrush	Dental floss
Toothpaste	Small tubes for liquids
Make-up and remover	Tissues
Hairbrush/comb	

Hygiene

Painkillers	Playing cards
Glasses	Pocket sewing kit
Contact lenses & solution	Sleeping bag (optional)
Travel journal and pen	Portable stove
Books	Cutlery
Sunglasses	Bowl/cup
Waterproof watch	
Beach towel/quick-dry towel	
Waterproof bag	
Water purifying bottle	
Sleep sack	
Earplugs	
Refillable bottles	
Travel neck pillow	

Miscellaneous

'HE WHO WOULD TRAVEL HAPPILY MUST TRAVEL LIGHT' ANTOINE DE ST-EXUPERY

Backpacking

	ESSENTIALS	ELECTRONICS
Basics	Passport	Camera and charger
	Boarding passes	Mobile phone and
	Foreign cash	charger
	Credit/ATM cards	Tablet and charger
	Maps/directions/itinerary	Headphones
	Guidebook material	Plug adapters
	First aid kit	Torch/headtorch and
	Travel insurance documents	batteries
	Repeat and travel medication	Waterproof pocket
	Folder for all documents	camera
	Large backpack	Back-up hard drive
	Small combination lock	
Clothes	Light jacket	Belt
	Waterproof coat	Thin socks
	Light jumpers	Underwear
	Thin hoodie	Sleepwear
	Casual shirts	Sun hat/cap
	Vest tops	Swimsuit
	T-shirts	Sarong/shawl
	Loose trousers	Hidden zipper belt
	Leggings	
	Shorts	
	Skirts	
	Dresses	
	Sandals	
	Flip-flops	
	Trainers/comfortable shoes	

'HE WHO WOULD TRAVEL HAPPILY MUST TRAVEL LIGHT' ANTOINE DE ST-EXUPERY

	DESTINATION:
	SPECIAL EVENTS:
	DAYS: WEATHER:

	ESSENTIALS	
Hygiene	Suncream and aftersun lotion	Hair products
	Body lotion/moisturiser	Disposable wipes
	Insect repellent	Sanitary products
	Deodorant	Nail file/clippers
	Perfume	Tweezers
	SPF lip balm	Bug spray
	Razor and shaving cream	Laundry kit: travel detergent, braided clothesline, sink-stopper
	Shampoo and conditioner	
	Soap/body wash	
	Toothbrush	Hand sanitizer
	Toothpaste	Dental floss
	Make-up and remover	Small tubes for liquids
	Hairbrush/comb	Tissues
Miscellaneous	Painkillers	Playing cards
	Glasses	Pocket sewing kit
	Contact lenses & solution	Sleeping bag (optional)
	Travel journal and pen	Portable stove
	Books	Cutlery
	Sunglasses	Bowl/cup
	Waterproof watch	
	Beach towel/quick-dry towel	
	Waterproof bag	
	Water purifying bottle	
	Sleep sack	
	Earplugs	
	Refillable bottles	
	Travel neck pillow	

'HE WHO WOULD TRAVEL HAPPILY MUST TRAVEL LIGHT' ANTOINE DE ST-EXUPERY

Backpacking

Basics	ESSENTIALS	ELECTRONICS
	Passport	Camera and charger
	Boarding passes	Mobile phone and
	Foreign cash	charger
	Credit/ATM cards	Tablet and charger
	Maps/directions/itinerary	Headphones
	Guidebook material	Plug adapters
	First aid kit	Torch/headtorch and
	Travel insurance documents	batteries
	Repeat and travel medication	Waterproof pocket
	Folder for all documents	camera
	Large backpack	Back-up hard drive
	Small combination lock	

Clothes		
	Light jacket	Belt
	Waterproof coat	Thin socks
	Light jumpers	Underwear
	Thin hoodie	Sleepwear
	Casual shirts	Sun hat/cap
	Vest tops	Swimsuit
	T-shirts	Sarong/shawl
	Loose trousers	Hidden zipper belt
	Leggings	
	Shorts	
	Skirts	
	Dresses	
	Sandals	
	Flip-flops	
	Trainers/comfortable shoes	

'HE WHO WOULD TRAVEL HAPPILY MUST TRAVEL LIGHT' ANTOINE DE ST-EXUPERY

	DESTINATION:	
	SPECIAL EVENTS:	
	DAYS: WEATHER:	

	ESSENTIALS	
Hygiene	Suncream and aftersun lotion	Hair products
	Body lotion/moisturiser	Disposable wipes
	Insect repellent	Sanitary products
	Deodorant	Nail file/clippers
	Perfume	Tweezers
	SPF lip balm	Bug spray
	Razor and shaving cream	Laundry kit: travel deter-
	Shampoo and conditioner	gent, braided clothes-
	Soap/body wash	line, sink-stopper
	Toothbrush	Hand sanitizer
	Toothpaste	Dental floss
	Make-up and remover	Small tubes for liquids
	Hairbrush/comb	Tissues
Miscellaneous	Painkillers	Playing cards
	Glasses	Pocket sewing kit
	Contact lenses & solution	Sleeping bag (optional)
	Travel journal and pen	Portable stove
	Books	Cutlery
	Sunglasses	Bowl/cup
	Waterproof watch	
	Beach towel/quick-dry towel	
	Waterproof bag	
	Water purifying bottle	
	Sleep sack	
	Earplugs	
	Refillable bottles	
	Travel neck pillow	

'HE WHO WOULD TRAVEL HAPPILY MUST TRAVEL LIGHT' ANTOINE DE ST-EXUPERY

Backpacking

DESTINATION:
SPECIAL EVENTS:
DAYS: WEATHER:

	ESSENTIALS	ELECTRONICS
Basics	Passport	Camera and charger
	Boarding passes	Mobile phone and
	Foreign cash	charger
	Credit/ATM cards	Tablet and charger
	Maps/directions/itinerary	Headphones
	Guidebook material	Plug adapters
	First aid kit	Torch/headtorch and
	Travel insurance documents	batteries
	Repeat and travel medication	Waterproof pocket
	Folder for all documents	camera
	Large backpack	Back-up hard drive
	Small combination lock	
Clothes	Light jacket	Belt
	Waterproof coat	Thin socks
	Light jumpers	Underwear
	Thin hoodie	Sleepwear
	Casual shirts	Sun hat/cap
	Vest tops	Swimsuit
	T-shirts	Sarong/shawl
	Loose trousers	Hidden zipper belt
	Leggings	
	Shorts	
	Skirts	
	Dresses	
	Sandals	
	Flip-flops	
	Trainers/comfortable shoes	

'HE WHO WOULD TRAVEL HAPPILY MUST TRAVEL LIGHT' ANTOINE DE ST-EXUPERY

	ESSENTIALS	
Hygiene	Suncream and aftersun	Hair products
	lotion	Disposable wipes
	Body lotion/moisturiser	Sanitary products
	Insect repellent	Nail file/clippers
	Deodorant	Tweezers
	Perfume	Bug spray
	SPF lip balm	Laundry kit: travel deter-
	Razor and shaving cream	gent, braided clothes-
	Shampoo and conditioner	line, sink-stopper
	Soap/body wash	Hand sanitizer
	Toothbrush	Dental floss
	Toothpaste	Small tubes for liquids
	Make-up and remover	Tissues
	Hairbrush/comb	
Miscellaneous	Painkillers	Playing cards
	Glasses	Pocket sewing kit
	Contact lenses & solution	Sleeping bag (optional)
	Travel journal and pen	Portable stove
	Books	Cutlery
	Sunglasses	Bowl/cup
	Waterproof watch	
	Beach towel/quick-dry towel	
	Waterproof bag	
	Water purifying bottle	
	Sleep sack	
	Earplugs	
	Refillable bottles	
	Travel neck pillow	

'HE WHO WOULD TRAVEL HAPPILY MUST TRAVEL LIGHT' ANTOINE DE ST-EXUPERY